GEO

Lexile: _____520L_____

AR/BL: _____

AR Points: _____

LET'S LOOK AT FEELINGS™

What I Look Like When I Am Surprised

Joanne Shepherd

The Rosen Publishing Group's
PowerStart Press™
New York

Published in 2004 by The Rosen Publishing Group, Inc.
29 East 21st Street, New York, NY 10010

First Edition

Book Design: Kim Sonsky
Photo Credits: All photos by Maura B. McConnell.

Library of Congress Cataloging-in-Publication Data

Shepherd, Joanne.
What I look like when I am surprised / Joanne Shepherd.— 1st ed.
    p. cm. — (Let's look at feelings)
Includes index.
Summary: Describes what different parts of the face look like when a person is surprised.
ISBN 1-4042-2511-0
1. Surprise in children—Juvenile literature. [1. Surprise. 2. Facial expression. 3. Emotions.] I.
Title. II. Series.
BF723.S87S44 2004
152.4—dc21

                                                2003005471

Manufactured in the United States of America

Contents

I am surprised.

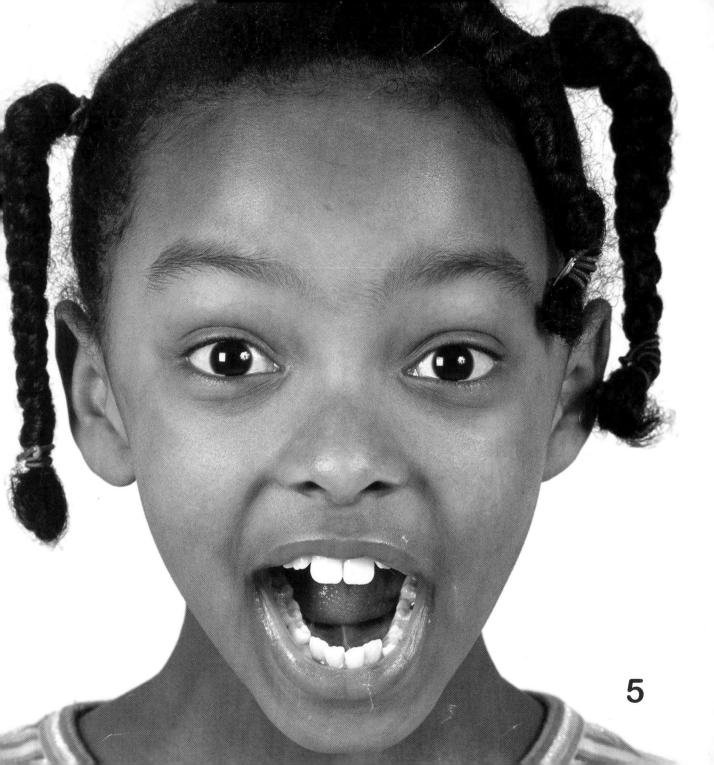

5

My eyebrows go up when I am surprised.

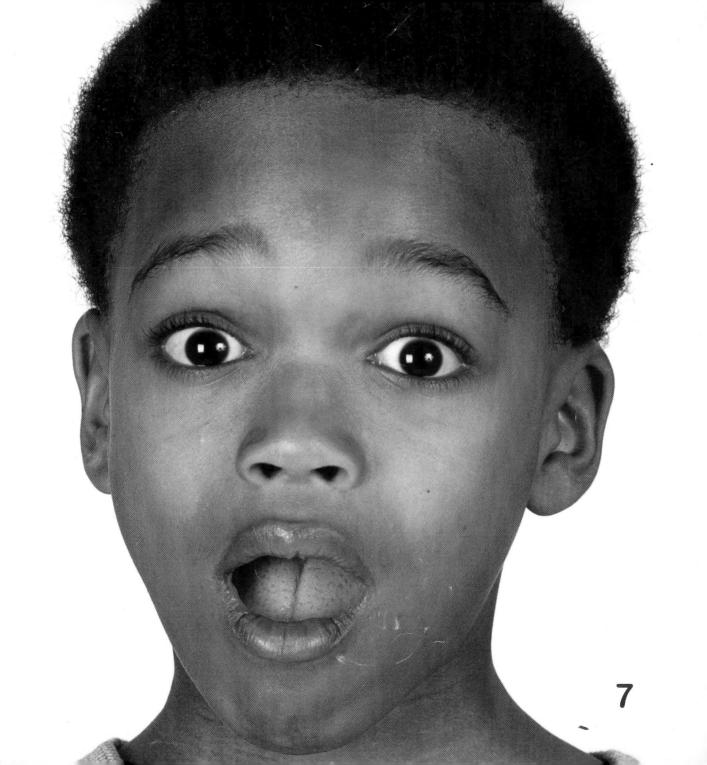

7

When I am surprised one eyebrow goes up and one goes down.

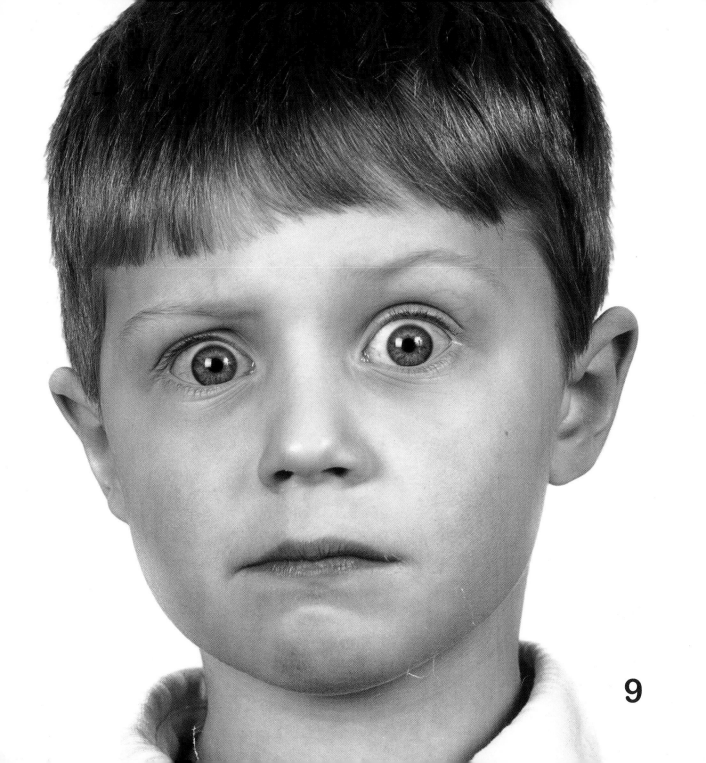

9

My mouth opens in a yell when I am surprised.

10

11

When I am surprised there are lines on each side of my mouth.

13

When I am surprised my chin drops.

15

You can see my teeth when
I am surprised.

17

My nostrils look bigger
when I am surprised.

19

My cheeks are high and round when I am surprised.

21

This is what I look like when I am surprised.

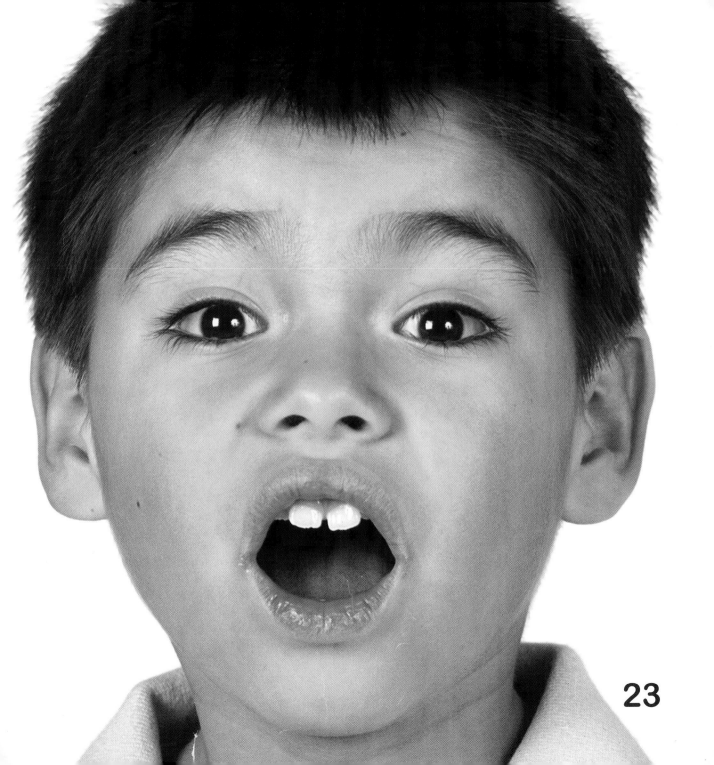

23

Words to Know

cheek

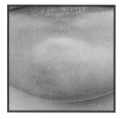

chin

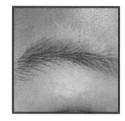

eyebrow

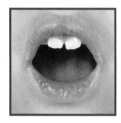

mouth

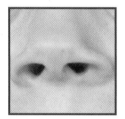

nostrils

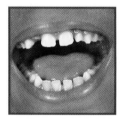

teeth

Index

Web Sites

Due to the changing nature of Internet links, PowerStart Press has developed an online list of Web sites related to the subject of this book. This site is updated regularly. Please use this link to access the list:

www.powerkidslinks.com/llafe/surpr/